I0182153

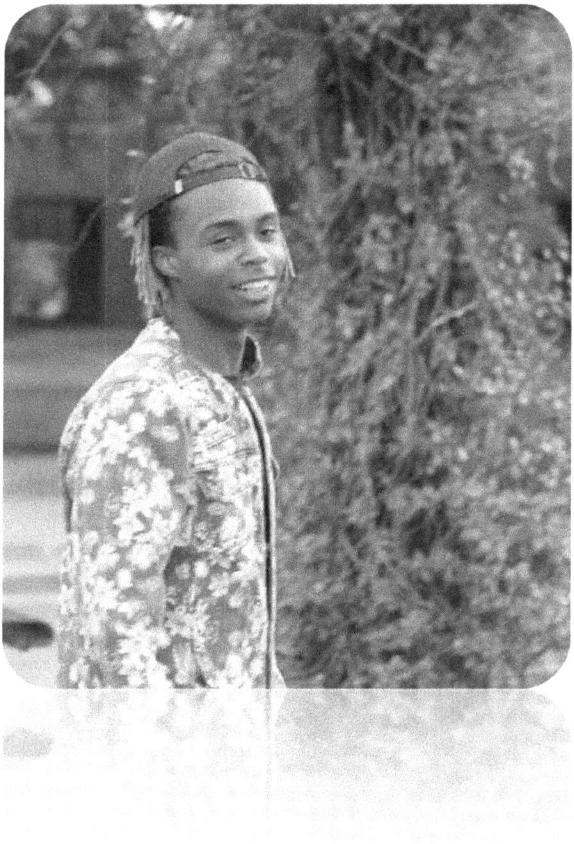

A Needed Vessel: Remembering Jalen

Published by Dreamers Arise, LLC

Houston, Texas 77379

A division of First Fruits Christian Center

Email: dreamersarisellc@gmail.com

© Copyright 2020

ISBN- 978-0-578-82714-8

All rights reserved. No part of this book may be reproduced or used in any manner whatsoever, without the express written permission of the publisher, except for the use of brief quotations in a book review.

Printed in the United States of America

First Printing, 2020

As children of God we are called to be the light. To shine upon many lives from the one who dwells within us. While some are called to do so inside of the four of walls of a church building, others are called to the community, the street, their jobs, their homes. Each of the stories you read are personal. They are all told from a different point of view, some laughter, others pain. Some express how they never knew personally, but was able to still express how their life was impacted by such a special vessel. One who was chosen by God to be a light. Although we see the end of his earthly vessel, each story bears witness to a life never ending.

Remembering the Life of Jalen

When I think of a memory of Jalen it would be when he asked to get baptized and the excitement he had about it. Not being forced by mom or others, he desired to be a part of the family of God. I also remember years later when I would travel and would stop at their home; he would make me feel welcome. I stayed for several nights with them. He made sure I was comfortable and ok. At their home in Huntsville, he would sit down in the living room and play games or watch a movie and would share with me what he would be watching. He talked to me about him wanting to be a doctor. I remember giving him a reference for his paperwork for scholarships. Jalen was that doctor, not in a hospital, but in the highways and byways of the world. He was a vessel used by God to draw others to Him through his ministry in the community, food pantry, and his home. I thank God that I was privileged to meet him along the way on this pilgrim journey in which we all are traveling.

With respect,

Pastor Carla Goree

He was a vessel used by God to draw others to Him through his ministry in the community, food pantry, and his home.

"Last memories of Jalen at the church"

We were at Spring Seat UMC church. Chassy and I were having one of our lil moments while ushering, assisting, and handing out fans, programs, etc. Her lil bro came to her rescue and said, "leave my sister alone." Our other auntie/ma had headed to the kitchen to fix plates toward the end of service. He also said later when service was over in the kitchen, "why you messing with my Aunt Lesia." Cuz Lee Lankford who was like another dad to me was sitting there laughing and watching the whole time. It was one of my fond memories of my lil cuz/bro he was always very protective of his sisters, brother, and fam.

Jalen McDuffie is my brother. I love you all so very much. Jalen McDuffie was a great person. We will always be here for you momma Nette.

Cuz/other sis Alesha & baby Honesty

I never really knew Jalen. Mostly because I was always kicked out of the picture room when the boys would play their video games. I always have one memory of him that I never seem to forget, though. It was Easter, and I had trouble looking for some eggs. Jalen saw me struggling and pointed out where some of the eggs were, practically cheating in order for me to get some candy. It seems silly now, but back then, I thought it was so admirable the way he didn't even hesitate to help someone out. It makes me sad that I never got to spend time with him, but I've learned just how great of a person he was, and I know my memory of him will always be a positive one.

Asha Bell

1st of all, I give all praises to God who is the head of my life, and thank Him for seeing another day. I'm Aunt Jean, Net's sister. Jalen has transitioned from this earth to his heavenly home and we have to do the same. It's time to wake up,& stay woke, Put aside hatred, backbiting, slander, grudges, gossip, and all other manners of evil and serve the Lord.

Here is my poem.

Dear Jalen
We love you, dear Jalen
We wanted you to stay
Our hearts are sad
and heavy
O, help us, Lord, we pray
We know that,
We'll meet again someday
Oh Lord, just help us
as we journey on this day
I know that Jalen is
happy, smiling over there
on the heavenly shores.
Oh the glory you will
reveal to us on that
beautiful, glorious morn
So for now, we will shed some tears,
And talk to our Master
who comforts and is
always near
So, the next time when
Your heart is breaking
And you're full of so much
despair
Look to the One who
is in the air, And
Know that Jalen is there
_ Home-

By
Wanda Jean Lankford Brewer
"Aunt Jean"

My brother was a sweet brother. He would always come into my room and check on me to make sure I was ok. He would bring me food as well. It was on my last birthday in August 2019, where he brought me cake and ice cream. It was just me and my momma. I miss everything about him.

Tribute to Jalen by

Jalen was a good-hearted brother. He always checked on me to make sure I was good. Jalen always brought me food and took care of me with my mother. Jalen was good and I miss him so much. Jalen's life matters! See you on the other side!

I love you forever Brother

Chassity McCoy

Jalen always had a smile on his face as a child teenager and man when I spoke to my lil cuz. I can still see when he was a baby with that mini baby bun hairstyle he had crawling around looking like somebody was about to get him. He and AJ running around in their little tighty whities lol. The last time I put eyes on him was at Tesha's house on thanksgiving day and he kept telling me how he wanted my red Jordan's I had on. That little twinkle in his eye like come on big cuz you don't need them shoes. My little cuz Jalen lol.

Keith Denard Lankford
Denard Lankford(Big Cousin)

There was a time when Jalen, helped me gain strength as a male in society. Through roughhousing and even when we played games, I would get upset, since Jalen would win every time. The only competition he had at the time was AJ. This taught me there will be obstacles in life that will seem near-impossible to overcome, but that is not an excuse to give up. Months ago when Jalen came to my house we played Tekken, a fighting game in which I have never beaten Jalen in. I pulled off I think two wins against him. Jalen was charismatic and enjoyed entertaining the crowd around him. Above all, he was a dear friend, who was strong, independent, and knew the life he wanted to live. Thank you for the lesson on standing firm on your feet and the understanding that life is tough and only those with a firm foundation can survive it. Enjoy your eternal vacation my brother in heaven. Thanks to you I can be firm in myself and withstand the changes of life with a smile.

Emarson Lankford
From MJ

I am Jalen's cousin Gabe. this is my speech-
Jalen is a very unique guy, it's like every time I saw him he had a different hair color. I remember he used to smack everyone on DOA, and even though he isn't with us physically, he is up there looking at us, smiling, not in pain, not just looking

Rest in peace Jay

-Gabe

Jalen was a very hard working young man who followed directions very well. I was his supposed supervisor and I never had any complaints about him or from him. I taught him to use "old blue" what we use at the pantry to move the food in and onto the pallet. Old Blue was the forklift type of machine. Jalen caught on his first try. He was always respectful, smiling, and working hard. He led on and showed the others how to work. Sometimes others would be breaking or such, but not Jalen. I have come inside many times and sometimes he would be the only person in there working the whole pantry by himself with that great smile and even greater customer service. He just loved helping. The customers were always asking "Who is that young man?" But that was just who he was. He would organize assembly for putting the food up and we always had it done quickly when he was there. He wasn't here on Tuesdays because he was working 2 jobs and going to Lone Star College to be a physician. His customer service was wonderful. Jalen was a hard-working, respectful young man whom all the other young men looked up to.

Gregory Jefferson

Tribute to Jalen Raschal McDuffie

The angel looked down from heaven one day.

The dear child for miles afar
And deep within the distance
They could see a shining star.

They know that very instant
That the star was there to give
So they took you up to heaven
Forever to remain

Look down on us from heaven
Keep us free from heart and pain
You'll always be within my heart
Until we meet again
I am going to miss your beautiful smile
Love,

Helen Houston

I remember back during one of the youth revivals at my Uncle Victor's church, myself, MJ, and Jalen were all taking turns freestyling to different rap beats. Expressing ourselves and how passionate we were about music and our different styles of rap flow is one of my never forgotten memories.

Holland Lankford

I remember Jalen and his brother AJ being babies about 2 and 3 years old. I was friends with his sister and we were in high school at the time. They used to always hang out of Tesha's bedroom window begging to go with us. Whenever we would, that's them places they used to always think Jalen was a girl. So handsome he was. I am still truly sad. RIH baby boy.

Holly Ramirez

Jalen was this charismatic, hilarious character that drew people to him. Jalen was not a follower, he did his own thing, and he didn't care who rocked with him and who didn't. I'll never forget about him talking to me about Majidah in one of our classes. This memory sticks out to me so much because I had never heard Jalen really talk about girls. And I remember asking him what he liked about her, and he got this little boyish grin on his face and said "I don't know, she's just DIFFERENT, like really different. She's cool." as he fiddled with his nametag in his hand. It's no shock to me they were together as long as they were. I don't think I've ever seen a more authentic match. I hope for strength for Majidah during this time. Jalen was an awesome person, and my heart is sad knowing that he is no longer here with the people he loved and cared about. However, one thing that I learned from listening to people speak at his funeral, is that he has touched so many people. Everyone that knew him has a piece of him, whether it's a memory, or something they learned from being around him, and we're taking that with us, to hold on to, and to share with others. Jalen McDuffie was a blessing, I'm thankful to have been able to know him for the few years I did.

Kaliya Williams

From the very first time I met Jalen his little personality stood out he had mad live for his big sis and little brother and everyone surrounded by him and that smile of his would brighten up anyone's day 🥺..I remember him and Aj coming to Tesha's for the summer's and visiting. One day I'm leaving my house and pops AJ and Jalen I'm like where are y'all going 🤷 why are y'all doing wat down here and with a big smile on their faces they said "we we're coming to say Hi " and little did they know I couldn't even call Tesha and be like their way down here at my house because I need that the fact they thought about me said a lot. I am so grateful I got to experience Jalen's sweet soul he will truly be missed by all he came into contact with they say the good die young and it doesn't seem fair but we never know our time and place rip young king 👑 😤 🥲 I took Spanish 1 with Jalen during Freshman year, that's when we became friends. Most people at school stuck with a specific group of personalities, but he got along with lots of different people. We shared tons of music and cracked jokes during class all the time. We didn't have any classes together after that, but we stayed in contact and I ate lunch at his table every now and then. He was very kind and unique and I know he made a lot of people happy with his presence.

-Kylie

I've lived in California the last 30yrs but I'm a Texan true & thru. When I heard about my young cousin's murder I was saddened and angered, two feelings.

I was sad because of all the endless pain caused by a senseless act by a lost and confused individual. Two kings never meet their queens, two families wrought with a cascade of emotions, two families saying goodbye (one to the grave, the other to a jail cell), two of everything.

I was doubly angry. Angry that my young cousin was in such a situation to begin with, angry that he even had people in his life/around him of such low caliber, angry that the shooter placed so little value on my cousin's life and even his own, angry that two lives albeit one is no more have eternally effected two families in unimaginable ways.
And for what.....

It's sad so many of our young black men still have no hope and find fake love in the streets. Why are we still not investing more in our own, reaching back, going back to help some-one like some-one helped us?

When will the eternal two's stop....
Cry and smile whilst remembering all that is good & all that is love.

LeMonte Lankford **(Jalen's cousin)**

**Cry and smile whilst remembering
all that is good & all that is**

Love

My last sweet memories....

Last mother's day weekend 2020 we made it to my mom's house. Everyone was so excited to see each other we tried to practice social distancing due to all this craziness with "rona"...we had plenty of Lysol spray, hand sanitizer and our masks...or we started out that way...I asked all my fam we hugging or elbowing, most gave me a big as always...When I saw my nephew it was like nothing had changed the same big hug, same bug smile 😁 I think I touched his hair and said oh it's nice did you do your own twist this time he said no a friend ..I Said well it looks "real nice he said thanks". If I had known that would be our last conversation I probably would have hugged even tighter and even longer...I remember the same big hug and smile right before they speed off...everyone said that's Jalen in his car.... 😘 ...I wasn't ready but I guess you drove and speed off to heaven so quickly...I'm still not gonna say goodbye, just see ya later nephew til I get there ♡♡♡ 😊🙏😇💋. Loving and missing you auntie ♡♡♡

Lesia Lankford/Lesia Hill

"Christmas memories of my babies"

For our family Johnson/Lankford, Christmas has always been a very special time for me and still is. We were taught at an early age the true meaning of Christmas is Christ. Of course, we also love our family time, the food and the gifts!!!My siblings and I have tried to pass on these traditions to our babies. Some of my fondest holiday memories are of my big sis Nanette aka Nette my third oldest sis ..but I call her my gorge sissy. She would sometimes arrive a lil late 😉 from Huntsville or other areas and say "do y'all want us, the food , or the gifts ..I don't have room for all"...You see she has a big giving heart like me and loves to give..."extra" like my baby gurl tells me all the time. Well my sweet young nephew Jalen and all my other babies loved to open their many gifts at their house...because we love to spoil our babies and give them a lil more than we had growing up...facts...they also couldn't wait to get to granddaddy/grandma's house to see what else they got, hang out with their cousins (aka other siblings because they were all so close) and then enjoy all the good food. I remember Jalen's sweet smile and I still see him in the picture room or video game room with all his cousins having fun until it was time to go home until the next holiday or family get together. These pictures and sweet memories will forever be in my heart....

Auntie/ma Lesia ...loves and misses you dearly 😇

"Our Last Thanksgiving supper"

I say this all the time: love your family and friends never. Miss an opportunity to tell them " I luv u " because we never know when it may be our last. Well during these Rona uncertain times" I believe more people have started doing that and "value our health hygiene and cleanliness , time and our families' '. I'm so very grateful that I'm a big hugger and say I love you all the time with my family. I have no regrets my nephew Jalen knew I loved him dearly. Our last Thanksgiving at my sweet oldest niece T-babys house we had a wonderful family Thanksgiving. She wouldn't let mem her mom or other aunties really do anything ,,,something I'm not used to 😊 She and my baby gurl took care of everything ..they honored us and let us rest and be served while I held on to my sweet lil calesy. She and Chassity were right by my side...auntie. proud moments. I realized what she was doing and felt ever more special until my hot boys 1&2 came. I love my handsome outstanding tall/talented (h.o,t ..incase y'all wondering why I/we call them that 😉). I'm so used to seeing them together. They were brothers and best friends ..you didn't see one without the other. I believe Jalen had his beautiful sweet girlfriend with him...they were such a cute couple. Of course like Christmas, Thanksgiving is and still is one of my favorite holidays . I love when we share what we are thankful for, our family prayer, family time and of course the food. This last thanksgiving with my Jalen and my big beautiful blessed fam I will hold oh so dear. We have lost loved ones over the years our big bro Jr, our daddae, aunts, uncles...but this loss was really devastating to my sissy, artie, tbaby, classy, aj, c.j, lele... even lil calesy and caleigh rae... all of us!!!!But, the sweet memories from that day that same big hug and smile when I saw them and when they left. I think they both mentioned in their remarks ``how important family is...they loved us all.." I also had a moment with him and my darniepooh boxing outside so I joined them for a moment. I showed them my moves and I learned kickboxing exercise class. I could tell by their faces they both were super surprised it made me feel food...auntie/ma proud moments....#priceless #timeless #thankful and blessed for all these sweet moments 😇🙏💪😗💨

"My Jalen 's graduation day"

Wow...graduations are special in my family. We love to celebrate each other's accomplishments. All our nephews/nieces are like our children...our other babies so we want to be there when we can...screaming, cheering the loudest (even though the program says ...wait until the end to applause 😄)...Of course, our family has grown over the years and we are all super busy and can't make it to everything all the time ...but when we do look out!!!! We have a saying ...several actually...I like to cheer "whoop whoop...we here!!!"...my lil/big bro says "let's do this!!!"or "All day" ...we mostly say before exercising or at a bball game or some sporting event but it works for everything !!!ijs 😉😄.,.Well on my/our Jalen's high school graduation I remember it well. We had just been at big bro aka tanks oldest son my mj aka cool boys 1&2 (cute/clever, outstanding, over achievers, loving/laughing...in case you were wondering) Duncanville H.S graduation the night before on a Friday ..we got up early Saturday morning rolled out to make a mad dash to Huntsville TX for his ....We got there found out where everyone was sitting...we wore green (we like to coordinate with the graduating class robe colors...it's our fam you might not understand 😄😄)... I believe bro bro had made this awesome poster ..he does it for his babies, my baby girl ree had a really cute one 2...Okay, I think it was my 1st time meeting lil c., her parents were already there ready to scream for her lil bro...sissy was overjoyed her baby joy graduating...last of her four children ...mom proud ♡♡♡So we anxiously await his name to be called JALEN RASHAD MCDUFFIE!!!!! We scream he hears us ...lolrotf... 😄😁 🚭 He gives that award winning smile poses with his diploma...We catch him after services give him hugs and congrats...take pics. All that...We go back to sissy to celebrate he loves all the gifts, cards with money and the food. I wrote in my card to my hot boy #2 spelled out the wonderful attributes of he and his big bro AJ #1...,#priceless memories #gr8 family memories and moments that live on in my ♡♡♡ til we meet again...auntie & fam...luv and miss you dearly I long for more but I'll wait til later 😇🍪😋

Thanks so much for all you are doing,

😇 J.G

So about yesterday I didn't take one pic, but my family always has my back. We celebrated the life of Jalen McDuffie. I/we called them the hot boys

H= Handsome & humorous

O= Outstanding and openly honest

T= Tall and talented

B= Bold and brilliant

O= Optimistic and over achievers

Y= Young and forever grateful

S= Smart and successful

We had so many milestones that occurred during this service. Faith over fear in attendance. No racial divides he impacted and reached people of all color inspired and encouraged his mom/siblings/family and so many young men and women to be unique selves. I wasn't ready to say goodbye but my spirit has a lil more peace. You always greeted me with a big hug smile and I'll forever be a very proud auntie for all blessed memories. Rest with the angels. I'll see you later baby.

Jalen McDuffie was MY little cousin. As he, and most of my younger cousins grew up, he became taller than me, but he was still a little cousin to me. I remember watching him grow and how much he admired his brother AJ and would often emulate him. However Jalen's own nature couldn't be hidden and his sweet spirit always shined through. As early as I can remember, he would always do or say something that expressed the genuine care in his heart. I hate that he's no longer here but I'm happy to know his kind and genuine spirit touched so many lives while he was here.

Love you Jalen,

Ma'Resia aka Cousin Ree Ree

My nephew was super smart and so much potential. I always tried to be a good example for him and my sons MJ and Holland loved to be around Jalen so much! Jalen made an impact on so many lives. Let's learn from this and be better each and every day.

Uncle Mitchell

Jalen aka Jae aka Jalo

I am the mother of Jalen Rashad McDuffie. He was scheduled to be born on 12/20/1998, but if you knew him he did not like to wait for some things. I am a married () head of the household woman that worked to provide for her 4 children while attending SHSU and achieving 2 bachelors. Jalen as a baby had beautiful green eyes and when he was displeased they became very dark green I thought that was amazing. His pediatrician told me that he was in the 93% and to keep his () channeled and I made sure to do that. Jalen and his brother A.J were both in the same category and I sometimes worked two jobs and roof over their heads to give them everything they needed and much of what they wanted. My eldest child Na'Jesla made a lot of this possible because she helped me with her brothers since she and her () Chanty were 12 years apart. Jalen as a child stopped nursing and drinking () milk at 8 months old and started walking () soon after that. I knew very early on he was special at the age of 2-3 he would come to me and () me 2's that made me go get Webster out and sure enough it would be in there, things such as sonic boom/blast/continental shifts, orbit of the sun in degrees to the earth, clean energy and etc. Now mind you he's not even in () yet.

But my eldest Jesha read to him in my belly and I was going to SHSU but still I thought that this was incredible and just reminded me of how special he was and I know that he was especially unique. So I kept them close, centered, and grounded best as I could. Church, family, school everything. He asked to be baptized as 8 years old and now mind you I would work a TDC all night take the kids to school, nap, cook, pick them up, get a CDL so I could drive the school bus and be in town to take them (Jalen) to karate class at 5 pm. I loved for a Saturday morning where I could sleep more than 30 minutes at a time. Jalen always was such a sweet child. He was raised to be a proud, independent, caring man to love () his family and to do your best at whatever you do and he did. I am so proud to be his earthly mother and I can't wait to see my beautiful baby again smiling. I love you Jae and miss you terribly.

Jalen Life Matters!

Missing You

Though I'm missing you

I'll find a way to go through

() Without, you were

My baby my strength and pride

Only God knows why still I must survive

Who ever knew that you had to leave

So suddenly so fast

How can it be but a sweet memory will all, all that we have left

Now that you're gone, every day I go on

But life is not the same

I'm so empty inside and my tears

I can't hid but I smile with every tear I cry, try and face the pain

() Here we so many thing that could said if time was on our side

Now that you're gone I can () you hear, so I'll smile with every tear I cry

How sweet were the **loses** you spare?

But I'll till the day till I'll you again I'll see you again

I'm missing you

Jalen life Matters!!

Mom

Jalen AKA Jalo My Young Prince

Jae as I'd called since he told me Mom my name is Jalen not JaLynn. I said well I will just call you Jae/ Jae Rock. How about that. We laughed about that. Jalen was born December 6, 1998. I drove myself with my sister, I kept telling her I knew something was wrong because I wasn't hurting. Long story short, the umbilical cord was wrapped around his neck twice. So I had major surgery and my baby boy weighed 10 pounds with green eyes. He fought coming in and going out. Jalen was the most gracious baby. He didn't cry a lot. He was such a beautiful baby. He was always quiet and smiling as he grew. I could already see he was unique, in a group setting. He would be in a space to himself playing or reading etc. The uniqueness unterrified as he got older. I could see his creativeness and independence only as a child. Before he started school he already knew his ABC's, counting, and how to write his name and his brothers as well. When he was born he topped the charts with a 95%. His pediatrician told me that he was special and unique but to keep his energy channeled. So I put him in a monastery before he started head start. When he got into regular school I would tell all his teachers to give him extra work because he was always ahead of the class. He was accepted into the gifted and talented program until he graduated. He was taking college courses in high school and was in the top 10% of his class at graduation. He never brought one book home. Yet he was always one the honor roll. Jalen played all sports and excelled in all. He first started out with soccer and Little Dribblers Basketball. As he got older, he played baseball and basketball. Later he played football until he broke his thumb. I never forgot he said, "Mom now look what happened." But he was good in it but that was it for Jalen. I told him I was exposing him to all sports to see what he likes. So then we started with karate and before that the YMCA in Palestine. Jalen was a boy scout and made it to beam before we had to relocate because of a promotion I had received at my job TDC. I took on another job by getting my CDL just so I could drive the school bus because I didn't want to pick them up from school and got back home then back to Madisonville. So by the time I got through with my route it was time to go to karate class. Jalen could karate! In Junior high, Mance Park, he ran track and played basketball. I was always so proud of Jalen and A&J. There, he achieved and excelled in whatever he did. Then there are the action figures from Spiderman to Power Ranger then Yugioh cards. Those things were expensive, but they were good kids so I bought the cards. In high school, he ended up with a stress spinal fracture in his back. I used to dress Jalen & A.J alike for as long as I could until one day Jalen said, "Mom I don't want to wear the same thing as A.J, I want to pick out my own clothes. That was Jalen wanting his own independence, individuality, and own sense of style and own sense of identity. So that was that there were no twins anymore. Jalen continued to excel in everything he did whether it was soccer, baseball, track, boy scouts, karate, school, basketball and later just life. My Jalen wanted to live and later from his friends and Mr. Gary was worried about him and my other kids. He was worried about me and my health as well as my daughter Chassity who also had only 25% of her heart functions (so the doctors say) After work Jalen would work out for 2 hours then run 8 miles everyday. Jalen wants to live and to be protective, progressive and to be more forward at all. Times Jalen never disrespect anyone that I know of. Jo know Jae was to love him. He cared about the future of his family. Jalen had long term goals he wanted to live life and to live life abundantly. Jalen Rashad McDuffie, my sweet green eye baby I love you so much I can't wait till you I see you and that beautiful smile.

My aunt Net and my mom Jean had 2 sets of kids, the older ones Tesha and Chassity; then A.J. and Jalen. My mom had my brother(Travis) and me, then my 2 sisters Kayla and Raylynn. Tesha was like a second mom to the boys and I was a second mom to the girls. We called them Brewer girls, and McDuffie boys. If you saw the boys, you saw the girls. I wrote an acrostic poem for him.

J-Joyful, as a person and to be around
A-Awesome
L-Loved by his family and friends
E-Eccentric he was unconventional
N-Nascent Meaning just coming into his own

♥ *your big Cousin Nikki*

I remember when my daughter Nanette had put the boys Jalen and AJ on a () school before they were old enough to attend early child school. She always was attempting to give her boys everything they needed with a special interest in education. I remember their mother told me that Jalen and AJ were placed special in mean separate playgrounds but they didn't play; they stood at the fence that separated them. AJ with tears in his eyes and they just stood there instead of playing touching each other's hands through the fence. I remember this story and I think that it () mountains of the love of these brothers. Jalen was so special to me. Jalen life matters! Grandmother will see you soon. I will always remember his beautiful smile and wonderful hugs with those beautiful eyes. Grandma loves you Jalen.

After one of my doctor's appointments, I went by to see Chassity who was sick. We arrived. I wasn't going to get it but I said to myself I'm going to see Chassity. So I got out of the vehicle and it seems like when I start walking I have to go (88 years young) Nanette and always accompanies me and they're always slowing me down. Nanette tries to hold me back, but I still just go alone. Anyways back to the jump up to go meet me. At this time Nanette comes out and Jalen began to tell her about how fast he was walking/running. I can see him imitating me. Nanette tells Jalen to do the impression. I said alright I'm going to get you. So Jalen said, "No, no I don't want grandma to get me".

Oletha Lankford(Jalen's Grandma)

Mr. Jaylan McDuffie, what can I say about this young man, who has gone to soon, we think in our human minute mind. But, We serve an almighty God who doesn't make a mistake and too just to be unjust, looked down the ages of time and saw his very own creation in the human form of Jaylan McDuffie, on loan to Nanette and Artie McDuffie, from December 6, 1998 to June 3, 2020. yrs. He saw that his assignment on earth had been done. He was obedient to his parents, pursued an education, Respectful and kind to others, believed that Jesus was the son of God, encouraged and helped the downtrodden and was even kind to his enemies. Jaylan loved his family and Loved all people. Jaylan didn't let struggles hinder him from pressing to pursuing a higher education at TSU. He was definitely on His way. I will stop here to say goodnight, a race well ran . We will keep your beautiful memories alive, tucked away in our hearts. Those we have held in our arms for a short while, we will hold in our hearts forever." Paul said, "None of us lives for ourselves alone, and none of us die for ourselves alone. If we live, we live for the Lord; and if we die we die for the Lord. Whether we live or die, we belong to the Lord. Romans 14: 7-8.

Onita Oliphant (Auntie)

Here is another beautiful story/memory about Jalen. About 2 weeks before Jalen passed, I was at home in Centerville talking to my sister, Jalen's Mom Nanette Mcduffie on the phone. She was at home in Huntsville. As we were on the phone I got in the car and headed to Madisonville to Brookshire brothers Grocery Store. Now right before I headed to Madisonville Jalen had gotten on the phone. My nephew talked me all the way to Brookshires. Nette said Jalen had taken the phone from her. Now that's not a big deal for my sisters because sometimes we can stay on the phone all day but as we all know some teenagers have no desire to stay on the phone with Family that long. So I was very surprised and pleased that Jalen talked with me that long but we had such an enjoyable conversation.

We talked among many other things about his TDCJ experiences because his mom and i had told him when he first started TDC that since he was kind of small, the inmates were going to try him. Jalen had simply said he was not worried. Now he was telling me that yes they did try him but he let them know in no uncertain terms who was in charge, and he recanted several instances to me of where, when and how he showed them who was in charge. I remember I was smiling and my heart was smiling because I was so proud of him at that moment. By this time I had arrived in Madisonville and I said well Jalen I'm about to go into the store so I'm going to let you go. Jalen said oh Aunt Pam you too buisie' too talk to me in the store? It was so funny that he still wanted to stay on the phone but I was so happy that he wanted to keep talking. I told Jalen I loved him and he was always going to be my baby even when he was being hardheaded and rude. So then Jalen said oh Aunt Pam so I'm going to be 50 years old baldheaded and still be your baby? And I said yes Jalen!! You will always be my baby!! As many other days my heart swelled with love for my nephew that day. He was his own person and he was a unique young man with a bright promising future. I thank God that he gave us that time for us to talk and for me to tell him I loved him because 2 weeks later he was gone. We love you and Miss you Jalen but God loved you best!!Rest in Heaven Nephew!!

So many memories of my nephew Jalen Mcduffie!! One precious memory when Jalen was younger maybe 10 or 12 we used to get him to dance like Beyonce. He and his brother were so Cute and he danced so good. So we would always say Jalen do Beyonce and he would immediately start dancing. He did this until he got a little older or the older kids started telling him he was dancing like a girl so then he wouldn't dance for us anymore 😊

Pamela Lankford

Jalen(Dark eyes)

When Jalen was about 4 or 5 years old he had the cutest little face and dark eyebrows. His mother Nanette had this things that sometimes when he was around people she would say Jay "Put them eyes on em", whenever she said that Jalen would immediately stop what he was doing drop his head, make a mean scowl with his eyebrows furrowed, and stare at whomever his mother was talking about, and give you the cutest little darkest look he could give. He was so cute and it was so funny.

I have a beautiful memory of my nephew's entrance into the world. On December 6, 1996 Nanette, Jalen's mother was in Huntsville 9 months pregnant with Jalen. She was close to her due date. Artie, Jalen's dad, has asked me to go stay with Nette since she was close to her due date and he had to go to work. Sometime that morning Nette started having labor pains. She and I headed to Conroe Hospital. (She had to drive because I wasn't a very good driver then) Once in the Maternity Ward the doctors checked Nette out and said it was time to deliver Jalen. It was approximately, 12 pm. After several hours of attempting to deliver Jalen, they finally informed us that there were some complications that they were trying to find out why Jalen was coming halfway down the birth canal and then going back up. I was in the waiting room and Artie had arrived by this time. After several hours the doctors finally realized every time Jalen attempted to come down the birth canal he was being stopped by the umbilical cord which was strangling him because it was wrapped around his neck! Once the doctors realized this they did what they had to do medically to take care of the issue. I don't remember the doctor's name but once they had effectively taken care of the situation with the umbilical cord, the doctors reassured Nette by her telling her "Don't worry Mrs. McDuffie, you've got a strong baby and he is going to be fine. She then promised Nette that Jalen would be in her arms by 4 pm. The doctor was true to her word and at approximately 4 pm a beautiful healthy baby was born to proud relieved parents Nanette and Artie Mcduffie. His name was Jalen.

My nephew had to fight to enter this world and due to senseless violence he had to fight his way out. But we his family know that he knows how much our hearts miss him and that he will forever be loved.

We love you Jalen.

I don't have a story, but when he and I worked at Promark together he was the sweetest kid ever. I told him I knew you Tesha and we would laugh and talk every day. We would always try to find a seat next to each other and we did more talking to each other than we did on the phone. I fell in love with him from day one I told him he didn't need to be working there because he should be on TV because he was so handsome and had a great personality. He will truly be missed by anybody who was ever blessed with his presence.

Quad Straughter

Jalen ——

Mom tells me we used to be best friends. We were the quiet ones, we really only spoke to each other (but I know we were really the coolest kids out of everyone else). Though I can't remember how we used to be and act when we were little, my favorite thing will always be that we used to be called "Jae and Ray." Kayla and AJ were close too, but never like us because we're the cool ones! As we got older, we didn't talk as much, but I remember going to your graduation and just being so excited for you. Seeing you out there, sitting through ALL THOSE PEOPLE just to hear your name being called and watching you walk across the stage. It was worth it, and I was and am so proud of you. You were so smart, and I knew everyone said it, but I was like yeah so am I, he can't be THAT smart. But I remember one time when we were in high school, I was at granny's house and I was trying to do math homework and I couldn't figure out this problem. So, granny called your house and they put you on the phone and I remember saying "No! Don't bother him, he's probably busy!" But next thing I knew, you were on the phone. So I told you what the problem was and how I had no idea how to solve it and I remember you helping me so quickly! & I was like what? And over the phone?! I was so happy though you'd never know and it was then I realized, "wow he may actually be smarter than me!" Another memory I have was when we had a family gathering, I have no idea what it was for but I remember you and AJ being there and I was like I didn't know y'all were here! But I got a hug when you arrived and when you left. and I remember saying, wow, I get TWO hugs?! We grew up a little differently & you had more obstacles to face than me, and yet you still turned out a pretty awesome person. I didn't know you like I thought I did, but from the people at your service, I got to know you a lot better. You touched so many people's lives and probably more than you even know. I was one of them, I never told you that. But you did, I found myself looking up to you and not even realizing how much your presence, smile, and just talking to you made me feel good.

Your smile lit up a room, and I hope people say the same thing about me because I'll say "thank you, I got it from my cousin." You will forever be in my heart, & I will always always always think of us as Jae and Ray. I can't wait to see you again, Rest In Peace, buddy. I'll love you forever.

- Ray ♥

Raylnn Brewer

I was brand new to Huntsville and went to my 2nd period history class and sat in the back next to a guy wearing a cool outfit who I had no idea would become my best friend. I was listening to Xavier wulf and not talking to anyone and you heard my music and asked if it was wulf. I had never met anyone who listened to him!! Instant connection. You showed me cool music videos and new artists and I showed you some of my favorites. From there it was always a battle between us and our teachers lol, and we had science together every year of high school. Haha I think back to physics class and I literally wouldn't have passed if it weren't for Jalen, I was constantly copying his homework! Our teacher would get so mad at us talking and laughing and me braiding your hair every day. It's crazy cuz you were really there for me as we grew up in life. You listened to my boy troubles and didn't let anything like that get between our friendship. I remember when I started picking you up for school every day and we would jam music so loud and pull up late to school EVERY DAY! Lmao going crazy in my minivan at 7 am. It's still hard to try to condense all of our memories into words because like I said, we literally grew up together. God I miss you so much. One of my all-time favorite memories is when I had a cheer competition in Montgomery and I begged you to come and you did!! Y'all were lost and couldn't find the gym and by the time y'all got there it was over but it was still so fun to see my best friend show up to support. Idk, to this day it meant a lot to me. I am so thankful that my last memory of you is so sweet. I came down to visit and we met for snow cones on my way out of town. You met my puppy Astro and he LOVED you lol. We talked about life and how things were going, big stuff and little stuff but it was so nice catching up with you. As we hugged and said goodbye you said "nah come here and give me one more hug because I don't know when I'll see you again" We hugged and held each other as 2 friends who no matter where life took us, that bond never broke. I talk about you all the time and it always warms my heart to hear people say they remember how close we were. Thanks for all the late night and summer adventures we took all around Texas, making memories, listening to music, putting each other on game, growing up and figuring out life together. Can't wait to see you again.

Rilee

Jalen R. McDuffie

He was a very handsome man, always had a smile on his face for most everyone he saw. He was loving, caring, and very helpful to other people. Anything you could ask him to help you do or do for you he did it with a smile. Never turned you down. He was very respectful all the time. I remember when I first met Jalen, I liked him at first sight. I told his mother "that is my child, my godchild", she said Jalen just smiled and laughed. That is how I looked at Jalen as my godchild. I loved him deeply and I'll always love him. Thank you Jalen.

Love your godmother,

Ruby Walker

To Our Brother,

We thought we would have time,

We thought we would have chances,

We thought that we could make plans,

but God had a plan for you.

Our hearts will always reserve a place for you.

A place for your light, your goodness and your smile.

Our love for you is infinite,

Sonya & Moniesha McDuffie

I had the pleasure of meeting Jalen the afternoon of Mother's Day when we went to Centerville, Tx. Victor and I had gone there to celebrate with his family. Before arriving at his Mother's home, we stopped at a local store to pick up a few items. Because I had never met Jalen I was not aware that the handsome gentleman that just passed the car as he left the store was Jalen. When Victor returned to the car, he mentioned that his nephew had just left the store. I told him that I indeed did see him as I noticed him because of his unique hair color. Very handsome! I did formally get introduced to him once we arrived at the house. He was such a respectful young man with a very calm disposition and the most beautiful eyes! I told him that I liked his hair color and he just smiled and said, "thank you." He greeted me with a kind hug & I will always cherish that moment. Much Love Jalen. Rest in Peace.

Sy.

Sy Belyeu(Uncle Victor's Fiancé)

No weapons formed against us shall prosper. Calm down and meditate. That's what I had to advise myself to do. Here was this young kid standing in front of me, no fear in his eyes just a clever spark, a twinkle if you will. We spared that day and it was no surprise to see the raw skill and talent that poured out of him, he was ever so smiling through the whole ordeal. Impressed was to say the least but it was like he and I where on the same wave link this was my family my little cousin. I was astounded as well as proud we laughed and kidded one another about what had just taken place. To some it probably saw it as just to people playing around, for me I saw it as a break through to something special. I didn't get to see him much but this time and another time before we made good positive energy. When we finished we made plans to link in the future and handshakes and brotherly hugs in towed. Nobody knows when our time is up but God. I just want to thank him now for time, I was allowed to spend those moments with Jalen.

Love you Jalen RIH

- his first cousin –
Thomas Darnell Lankford aka Bookie

The first time I met Jalen was during the summer while he was finishing up high school. The bond that I saw him share with CJ was amazing. The time he spent and respect he gave his nephew will go unmatched. Just like the time they spent on their games.

He was a young man with a light of eagerness and a humble spirit. This was the perfect balance of who he was a brother and protector.

The time that I saw him he was always willing to lend a helping hand with the tasks to be done at the home and anything else, because nothing was too small or beneath him.

His positive attitude opened more doors for him and once he was inside his work ethic made sure he had a seat at the table. Even though he is no longer with us his spirit will continue to be here and me we all take a page from the book of lessons he taught us.

Toi Lloyd

My last encounter with Jalen was at our family reunion. I had asked him what was going on in his world and he stated that he was no longer working for TDCJ. I of course inquired why and Jalen told me that it was a lot of crazy incidents that had happened in the prison and he had to leave to get his mind right and figure out his next plan of action. I encouraged him to take his time and everything will work out. Even though our conversation was brief, it was good to know that my lil cousin was trying to stay on the right side of life and think about the future in a positive way. It hurts that his earthly essence was disrupted before it had a chance to mature and blossom...... but God makes the final call on such things. R. I.H. Jalen.

Travis Lankford:

The Lord didn't bless me with a 2 pm, but Jalen was truly a young man. I would have loved to be my boy and now. He was so respectful and kind and helped any woman. I thank his mother for a well-rounded child that we had a short time to know and love.
I love you

Verna Cole

Jalen,

For all my Family and friends that know me - know that I love the kids especially my nieces and nephews. I have spent my entire life trying to be there for them all 15 nieces and nephews and 14 great nieces and nephews. I have always and will continue to have a special place in my heart for Jalen and AJ. See Jalen and AJ needed me more than the others due to the fact their father didn't stick around. They needed him the most. My sister did all she could to raise these 2 boys and she would always ask me to be involved in their life and help them become the men we all knew they could be. So with that being said Jalen spent several summers with me and I would take him to Youth revivals at my church and pour into him as much as I could with the time he was with me. I always told Jalen to take care of the people that have been there for him, especially his Mom and sisters. I would always tell him that you don't want to be a burden to your Mother and you should always want to make sure she is good before anything else since she has broken her back to provide for you! We would always talk about that and Jalen knew if at any time I felt he was doing something that wasn't right I would let him know and I think he appreciated me for that. I remember some of our last text messages and conversations - I could tell he was getting it together and some of the things I had been talking to him about were starting to sink in. In our last conversation over the phone we had a heated conversation and he stood toe to toe with me man to man and tried his best to defend his position and I will always respect him for that. At the end of the conversation he told me Unc you are right I didn't even think of that and I appreciate you calling me out on it. I told him I loved him and he told me he loved me too! The last time I saw my nephew Jalen alive was Mother's Day weekend and we didn't talk a lot that day but as always he gave me that big and warm smile and we hugged and I will always remember that. Jalen your spirit and smile will LIVE ON - continue to be our angel and look over your Mother, brother, and sisters they are going to need to feel your spirit to help them deal with your absence here on earth; but we as believers know that to be absent from the body is to be present with the LORD!

Here are a couple of the last text messages I had with my nephew Jalen McDuffie - Love ya boy!

December 2, 2019

Jalen text to me: Unc it just be hard on this side and I be trying to a lot of stuff on my own

My response: That's part of becoming a man Jalen we all went thru it just stay focused on the goal and don't disrespect the people that try to help you especially your Momma

Jalen: I'm gonna put my family in a better place

My response: That's what I want to hear, your Unc needs some help!

Jalen: Don't worry in two years from now I plan to have some thousands from this empire I'm building....LOL n yeah it's all above water

My response: Okay cool

Jalen: It's gonna be beautiful and I already know what I need to do......all is left is to do it!

My response: I have always believed in you and AJ - I know you have it in you! Just handle your business

Jalen: That's right

December 6, 2019

My text to Jalen: Happy 21st Birthday Jalen!!! Unc loves you and wants nothing but the best for you!!! Enjoy becoming a MAN!!!

Jalen: LOL(I can see that smile) appreciate Unc I hope you have a blessed day....

Your Unc - Victor Lankford

Jalen:

Victor Lankford

...More than an Empire, now, a Mansion